W9-CMR-818

THE HERO IN MY POCKET

By: Marlene Lee
Cover and Graphic Design: Reakha Janus
Artwork by Children

A portion of the proceeds from book sales will be donated to selected organizations that support military families.

Early Light Press, LLC

Copyright © 2005 by Marlene Lee

All rights reserved. Chapter "HERO PAGES" may be reproduced for individual personal use only. For other than individual personal use, such as, but not limited to, groups, organizations, commercial enterprises, schools, etc., prior written permission must be obtained from the author c/o Early Light Press. Include organization name, goals, quantity desired, and contact information. Otherwise, no part of this publication may be used or reproduced, stored in a retrieval system, or transmitted, in any form or by any means, electronic, mechanical, photocopying, recording, etc., without prior written permission from the author c/o Early Light Press.

Artwork and pictures are used throughout the book for artistic impression only.

Cover and graphic design by:
Reakha Janus, Janus Consulting, Inc.
www.myjanus.com

For information about ordering *The Hero in My Pocket,* visit Internet website:

www.earlylightpress.com

Early Light Press, LLC
P. O. Box 317
Boyds, MD 20841-0317

ISBN: 1-4196-0152-0
First printing: January 2005; Second printing: April 2005
This book was written, printed, and published in the USA.

Table of Contents

Sam, age 8

Preface

Dear _____ ,

I'm sorry I cannot recall your name, but I doubt you would remember me anyway.

I was the Red Cross volunteer assigned to work with you the night you awaited your husband's air evac flight from Landstuhl to another premier military medical facility Stateside. Miracles of military medicine seemed to be standard procedure for injured soldiers.

But, your soldier, your National Guardsman, your husband, the father of your adorable children, was not airlifted for long-term medical treatment. He was scheduled to arrive, staying only long enough for final goodbye's.

You were, I realized in prayerful silence…a widow-to-be.

My years of Red Cross experience suddenly seemed insufficient; training had not included supporting those facing imminent widowhood. Nor were my corporate business skills applicable to the art of being "in the moment" with a widow-to-be.

So, it was as a mother and as a confidante to dying loved ones, that I sensed your many fears. I noticed how you tried to hide your trembling hands, and witnessed the darting pain in your eyes and strain in your voice. I wanted to march down the hallway and tell those people whom we could hear talking and laughing to be quiet! Stop laughing! Don't you know this young woman's world is being torn apart!

I continually asked myself: how might I salve but a sliver of the pain?

I remember, _____ , how the pictures of your children made us both smile. We talked about them for quite awhile. When you were finally allowed in to see your husband, I knew a new chapter of life would begin.

All the way home from my shift that night, I cried. For you, trying to be so brave. For your husband, who would give his life for our country. For the parents and siblings whose hearts would evermore ache. For your children whose pictured smiling faces would soon be streaked with tears and wrought with confusion.

And, for the realization that you could have been my daughter-in-law who, like me and countless others with loved ones deployed, fear the phone call that was your reality. Fear the sound of a car door slamming. Fear the sound of the doorbell ringing.

Please know that you, your husband, and your children inspired me, motivated me, and sustained me during the entire research and writing of this book.

Surely, _____ , I could have been a better volunteer if I knew then what I know now after graduate studies in Thanatology (the sociology and psychology of death, dying, and bereavement) at Hood College, and after pursuing independent research on children whose losses tend to be uniquely compounded after the death of their loved one who served in the United States Armed Forces.

Alas, from your loss I hope that others might accept *The Hero in My Pocket* to salve but a sliver of the pain.

Kind regards to you and your children.

Sincerely,

Marlene Lee
January 20, 2005

Note To Adult Caregivers

When one or both parents serve on active duty for the Armed Forces of the United States of America, military family members endure separations, stepped-up duty on the homefront, and expectations from society to "soldier on." Thus, the family, including the children, should be viewed, albeit in an auxiliary manner, as serving and supporting the nation, too.

Jillian, age 5½

Children in military families, known for their remarkable resilience, often develop an understanding of loss and renewal based on moving, relocating, and intermittent absences. The death of a military parent however, sets in motion a rapid succession of losses, particularly compared to the civilian (non-military) community.

The goal of this book is to facilitate understanding, communication, and interaction with a child following the death of the child's loved one who served in the U.S. military. Open-ended questions help promote discussion, and HERO PAGES encourage verbal and non-verbal expression of thoughts and feelings.

In *The Hero in My Pocket*, the "Special Hero" who has died is the father of two children, a girl and a boy, ages seven and 10 years, respectively. The children exhibit age-appropriate, developmental aspects of bereavement making the book suitable for reading with the age group six to 12 years.

Although the parent/child relationship is primary in this story, I have termed the phrases "Special Hero" and "Special Heroine" to reinforce the applicability of loss and remembrance to a multitude of relationships: parent, grandparent, sibling, other relative, in-law, friend, fictive kinship (significant relationship outside of the family), etc. In mourning loss, the significance given the relationship by the survivor is a key factor, more so than any familial, societal, or legal name for the relationship.

This book incorporates the whole language approach to reading, meaning all of the language skills are encouraged: listening, thinking, reading, speaking, and writing or drawing. With short chapters and HERO PAGES for drawing or writing, children can set the pace at which they progress through the book. Discussions may be painful, cathartic, or any other facet of emotion. Note that Chapter 6, *Shades of Red and Blue,* is the longest chapter highlighting emotions.

Wishing you a heartfelt connection through sharing and communication.

Jillian, age 5½

Acknowledgments

My heartfelt appreciation to the soldiers and their loved ones who shared with me their stories about what *really* matters in life.

Saying "thank you" does not adequately acknowledge my gratitude for the contribution Morten G. Ender, Ph.D., had on improving the book. As if teaching cadets at West Point, conducting valuable research, writing, and having a family are not enough to keep him busy, along comes a graduate student asking to analyze and discuss his research.

Reakha Janus, President, Janus Consulting, Inc., undertook the publishing process for this book with a passion that rivaled my own, perhaps propelled by the murder of her beloved cousin in 2002. Reakha's professionalism, publishing expertise and creativity, and generosity of time and friendship brought this book to its visual life. I am most grateful.

Indeed, every picture does tell a story. I thank the many children who eagerly created artwork as their way of supporting the children who will read this book. A special thanks, too, to those who shared photos. And, a collective thank you to the many friends and family near and far who believed in this project with me.

Thankfully, Andrea Warnick was my semester-long sounding board for discussing ideas for the book. Her remarkable work with ill and dying children and their families will continue to inspire others and enable her to change the future of death education.

Warm thanks and best wishes to Chaplain (Colonel, U.S. Army, Retired) Jack N. Anderson and Cheryl Parrott who read and commented on multiple drafts of the book even in the midst of planning their wedding.

I appreciate that Christine Allison, American Red Cross volunteer and instructor extraordinaire, encouraged me to take on leadership roles with the Red Cross. The Red Cross needs more people like Christine.

Last, but really first, Gregory and Cara, you epitomize what it means to be an Army team: strong, proud, side-by-side taking care of soldiers and their family members. Your service led me to mine – thank you with love always.

ml

This Women's Army Corps Lieutenant outranked her Army Air Corps husband when they married in the 1940's.

This soldier's great-great-grandfather served in the Civil War and his son-in-law served in the Global War on Terror.

High-tech holiday greetings in 2004.

More than 50 years after the USMA 1953 graduate branched Air Force, he and his bride have three children, nine grandchildren, and two great-grandchildren.

A lifetime of selfless service to the Army and the Army Reserves awaited this couple who married in the 1950's.

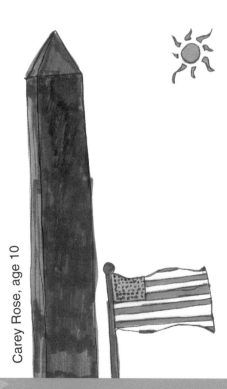

Carey Rose, age 10

Chapter 1
Special Hero

Greg and Grace's dad is their Special Hero.

Or rather, he was their Special Hero.

But wait, he still is their Special Hero.

Let me explain…

Greg was 10 years old and Grace was seven (plus one-half, as she will remind you) when their father was killed serving in the United States Armed Forces.

How strange to suddenly hear people talk about their father in the past. "He *served* our country with pride," said his commanding officer.

"We all *looked* up to him," said his friends in the unit.

Everyone agreed, "He *was* a man of solid values and faith. His family meant everything to him."

"My dad loved the military," Greg thought. "How could this happen to *me*? To *my* dad? To *my* family?"

Painfully and silently, Greg understood his dad was not "away" on a trip or training. His dad was not temporarily deployed. This was definitely not temporary.

Grace's questions dripped salty tears of sadness. Now, who would help her learn to swim? Explore new bike paths? And read stories using funny voices?

Over and over, Grace asked her mother to tell her what had happened, as if to make sure it was true.

It was. And it is.

Greg and Grace soon discovered that children in military families face many kinds of losses when their military parent dies.

With this story, Greg and Grace share their grief and remember their father – their Special Hero. They invite you to do the same for your Special Hero or Special Heroine. This book is for more than reading; it is also for drawing, writing, sharing, and remembering.

Savannah, age 4½

Who is your Special Hero or Special Heroine?

Is it your mother or your father?

Big brother or sister?

Is it your grandfather or grandmother?

Aunt or uncle?

Your favorite cousin?

A friend who is loved like family?

Write your Special Hero or Special Heroine's name here:

_____

Write your Special Hero or Special Heroine's military service branch here: _____

Chapter 2
Living with History

Greg and Grace were proud of their dad in his crisp military uniform. From the top of his hat to the shine on his shoes, his uniform was a living history lesson.

Colorful ribbons were reminders of places their father had served and honors he earned protecting our country's freedoms in peacetime and in war.

His patches and insignia were symbols passed down from generations of brave men and women before him. Even the crest on the buttons carried an historical meaning.

Camouflage uniforms signaled a history of their own. With clever colors and patterns…for jungles…for deserts…for lands of snow and sky.

Sturdy boots paired with camouflage uniforms…

Boots for marching.

Boots for climbing.

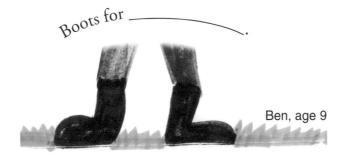

Boots for ———.

Ben, age 9

(What do you think? Fill in the blank above.)

Greg and Grace especially liked that their father's camouflage jacket had lots and lots of pockets. Why? Because when Greg and Grace's dad traveled away from home, he promised each of them:

"Your heart is in my pocket so I can take your love with me wherever I go."

Greg, age 7

Sometimes their dad's training had lasted days or weeks. Sometimes months. A full deployment could even last a year or more.

Luckily, camouflage jackets have lots and lots of pockets!

Greg and Grace invite you to use the following HERO PAGE to draw or write about your Special Hero's uniform or military history.

HERO PAGE

Jillian, age 5½

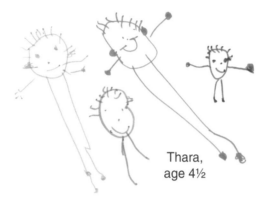

Thara,
age 4½

Chapter 3
Community of One

Greg and Grace's non-military, or civilian, friends did not always understand that absences – sometimes short, sometimes long – are a normal part of military family life. However, Greg and Grace were fortunate because most of their friends were "military brats" and they did understand. You know, kids from military families affectionately call each other military brats for living here and there and everywhere!

Military brats swap stories about living in different places in the United States and in foreign countries, such as Japan, Germany, and Italy. And military brats know that moving means leaving your school, your teachers, your friends, and your place of worship…then…moving forward and gaining a new school, new teachers, new friends, and new place of worship.

Moving! Adventure! Exploration! Excitement!

Moving! Butterflies in your tummy! Buckets of tears on your pillow! Saying goodbye!

Actually, saying goodbye to a military family friend doesn't necessarily mean you won't see them again. Greg and Grace's friends, Rosa, Laurie, and Lorenzo, lived near each other at two different bases. "See you later!" seemed better than "Goodbye!"

Savannah, age 4½

Have you ever had an old friend show up in your new school or housing area?

Because military families share similar experiences with moving and traveling, Greg and Grace's parents believed this shared "culture" helped children and grown-ups make new friends quickly.

Before when they had moved, Greg and Grace depended on their dad, their mom, and each other…and the furry friendliness of their family dog, Scout.

Erin, age 8

As a family, they had moved together, stayed together, explored together, and laughed and cried together. For years, they had also depended on the tight-knit community of military families. They would now move away from their military roots and into civilian life, permanently.

Greg and Grace felt very sad about moving without their dad. His death still echoed loudly in the empty places in their hearts. And sometimes in their dreams at night.

Yes, this move would be different. Very different. Where would they live? What would moving be like without their dad? And, what would it be like to move away from their military community?

G. George, age 9

Greg and Grace moved several times as a military family. On the following HERO PAGE draw or write about your own experience with moving or traveling.

HERO PAGE

Skylar, age 12

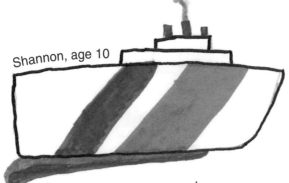

Coast Gaard

Shannon, age 10

I am really proud of my mom because she works in the Coast Gaard.

Chapter 4
Pocket Full of Memories

To prepare for the move to civilian life, Greg, Grace, and their mom talked about military families who live and go to school in civilian communities. National Guard and Reserve families sometimes live far from the nearest military post – and from each other.

Greg, age 7

Army, Navy, Marine, Coast Guard, Air Force, and Merchant Marine families do live in civilian communities, and in families with two parents, one parent, divorced parents, or deployed parents. Some kids live with their grandparents.

Well, being only seven (and one-half, remember), Grace worried, "How will my dad know where to find me when we move?"

Right away, Greg understood his younger sister's concern. He comforted himself by silently talking about everything and anything to his father, as though he were still alive. Greg believed his dad was listening and watching over him and would always be alive in his heart and in his memories.

"I have an idea!" Greg shouted. He asked his mom for one of his father's old camouflage jackets.

When Greg slid his arms through the too-big sleeves, the jacket wrapped around the son like a big, fatherly bear hug. The faint scent of his father's aftershave on the collar instantly flooded Greg's mind with memories of his dad: camping out and hiking mountain trails together.

For a minute, or maybe two or three, Greg stood suspended in time – his memories at full attention, his heart at half-mast.

Skylar, age 12

Then, with their mom's permission, Greg and Grace each cut a pocket from their dad's old camouflage jacket.

Together, Greg and Grace made a pledge to their dad. It was the exact pledge he had made to them many times:

"Your heart is in my pocket so I can take your love with me wherever I go."

Greg and Grace's mom encouraged the children to choose mementos from their father's personal belongings to keep for themselves. Grace selected several of her dad's favorite military coins.

"The pocket! It's the perfect treasure holder," Grace exclaimed. The oversized coins clinked and clanked to the bottom of her camouflage pocket.

Greg selected several pieces of his father's brass rank insignia as mementos. He wanted to save the insignia forever and never lose it.

Of course, in the day-to-day life of a kid, it is not practical to carry a camouflage pocket everywhere. So, Greg and Grace decided to use whatever pocket they had on their clothing to carry their dad's love with them. And, if the day's clothing (or their pajamas) did not have pockets, then they would tuck their love for their dad – their Special Hero – in the pocket of…

"My heart!" Greg and Grace shouted at the same time.

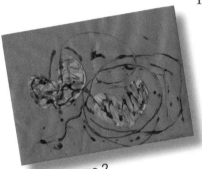

Matthew, age 2

That's it! The pocket of my heart. No matter where they moved to, now and forever, the pocket of each child's heart would be the safest place of all for their father's love.

Emily, age 3

Greg and Grace invite you to use the following HERO PAGE to draw or write about a personal or "hand-me-down" memory of your Special Hero.

HERO PAGE

Sam, age 8

Chapter 5
Like New

Along with their mom, Greg, Grace, and Scout moved in with their grandparents for awhile. They were welcomed at their grandparents' place of worship. Before the moving trucks even arrived, Greg and Grace had transferred into the neighborhood school!

Soon, they moved again. Although their home was not brand new, it was new to them. Mom looked for a job and promised to find new soccer teams for Greg and Grace to join. Yes, things were changing quickly. Familiar activities would help them settle in. Still…

Why did this move feel strange compared to other moves? Shouldn't they be used to the newness of moving?

In the dawn's early light of each new day, the kitchen seemed bright and fresh. In the evening's setting sun however, dinnertime was a painful nightly reminder that their dad was not there. And he would not be coming home like he used to after a deployment.

Jillian, age 5½

Yet, dinnertime remained a family routine. They continued the traditions of sharing and listening to each other and keeping the television turned off during mealtime. They thought their dad would approve.

Grace glanced at the big calendar on the wall. She loved math and kept track of the months and days until her birthday. Pushing her food slowly around her plate, Grace wondered, "What will my birthday party be like without Dad?"

The calendar on the wall marked time with activities, appointments, and important dates. But, grief doesn't have a regular calendar like the rest of life does. A grief calendar marks a year of "firsts." For example, moving without their father was a "first," a difficult one at that.

Still to come: their "first holidays" without him, their "first birthdays," and their "first Father's Day." From now on, Memorial Day and Veterans' Day would be flagged as special days for remembering.

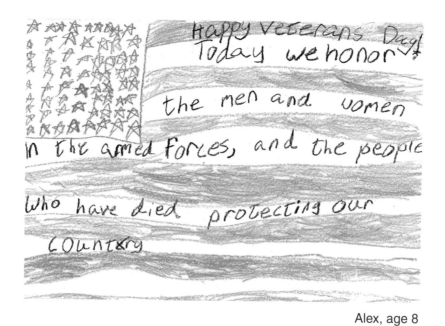

Happy Veterans Day! Today we honor the men and women in the armed forces, and the people who have died protecting our country.

Alex, age 8

Below are things that are new to Greg and Grace in their new town and things that are the same. What can you add for Greg and Grace or for yourself?

Sam, age 8

New	Same
Neighbors	Scout, the family dog
School	Favorite books
Bike paths	Bicycles
Place of worship	Faith

Thara, age 4½

Greg and Grace invite you to use the following HERO PAGE to draw or write about a special occasion or holiday to honor and remember your Special Hero.

HERO PAGE

Sinead, age 10

Chapter 6
Shades of Red and Blue

Whenever Greg and Grace's dad had been deployed, Greg had taken over his dad's responsibilities for walking the dog. In the new neighborhood, Greg, Grace, and their Mom all walked Scout together. Scout led the way with his head held high and his tail wagging.

Megan, age 4

After a few minutes, their Mom asked, "So, what do you think about the new school?"

As though it had been on his mind at that very instant, Greg answered quickly. "Different."

"What do you mean by different?" Mom responded.

Greg searched for the right words because it wasn't simple to explain. On the inside, he felt as though other kids could tell just by looking at him – on the outside – that his father was dead. He compared it to having a target on his shirt that everyone could see: big, round, and colorful.

red

Savannah, age 4½

His mother assured him that you couldn't tell just by looking at someone that their loved one had died. Maybe so, thought Greg, but he had yet another idea about feeling different.

As Greg tried to speak, he reeled in Scout's leash and patted him on the head. Surely, Scout missed their Dad, too. They all continued walking. Then, Greg's voice squeaked in an angry whisper, "Except mine."

"Except what?" his mother asked softly as she stepped closer, ready to listen further.

Greg's voice rose, "Except *MINE*. Everyone else's dad is alive and living. Except *MINE!* It's *NOT* fair!" There, he'd said it! Aloud. Angry.

Grace immediately echoed Greg, "Yeah, it's *NOT* fair! We're the only ones without a dad!"

Anger was bubbling up and oozing out.

Nicole, age 4

Sadness, too. When someone you love dies, the emotions that follow can be so unpredictable. For days. For weeks. For months.

Fresh tears glistened on their Mom's face. Gently, she hugged her children in close to her until the three of them were side-by-side-by-side on the sidewalk. She said, "It's okay to be angry, kids. I feel angry sometimes, too. And sad. We're all hurting inside."

She continued, "Let's talk about what to do with the energy of anger to get it out. And let it go."

"Ride my bike," Greg said.

"Play video games!" Grace added. "And jump rope…or play jacks."

Hockey by Andrew, age 6½ plus ¾

Physical activity is one sure way to help let go of anger. Go ahead, bounce a ball, ride a bike, take a walk! Try going to a sporting event and yelling for your favorite team!

What about…putting anger to paper?
Try drawing or writing in a journal.

What about…going on a journey?
Try reading a book or a map.

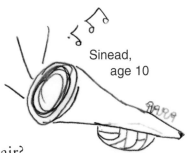

Sinead, age 10

What about…sending anger out into the air?
Try singing or playing a musical instrument.

What about…sharing your feelings?
Try talking to a good friend or a trusted adult.

Their mom explained, "Feelings can be confusing. I talk about my feelings with my sister. Talking helps to sort out what those feelings really are."

"Kids," she continued, "talking isn't just for grown-ups. You're not alone, even though it feels that way at times." She touched the dog tags she now wore as a memento necklace and said, "I don't know what I would do without you. Please remember that no matter what you are feeling, it is not OK to hurt yourself or anyone else."

Megan, age 4

Having reached their front door, Greg unhooked Scout's leash and had something else to say about feelings: "I don't like when kids keep asking, 'Where's your dad?'"

Grace agreed, "Totally annoying! Some kids act so weird when they find out Dad died."

Greg said, "Maybe they think if our dad died…and it happened to us…that it could happen to them." He paused. "And that would be scary for them, too."

Their mom listened to Greg and Grace's feelings and said, "It's hard to know what to say. People use different words that mean the same thing as death or died."

Home going

Loss

Pass on

Pass away

She asked, "I wonder if it would help to practice what to say when kids or grown-ups ask about your dad?"

Ben, age 9

Rehearsing what to say and how to say it just might help with those awkward moments, stares, or "Sorry's." Practicing seemed hard at first, but it helped.

When their dad's parents heard about "practice" they wanted to practice, too. There, in the comfort and security of the children's own home, everyone had time to think about their answers.

They looked at pictures, too. Their father's father began to tell stories about other relatives who had served. Then, their father's mother started to share too, telling the children cute stories about their father as a young boy.

Megan, age 4

Slowly, everyone started to smile. And laugh a little. Yes, laugh.

Hadn't they just been mad? And sad? Who knew you could laugh when your heart hurt so much?

Greg and Grace's mom spoke the truth for the children by saying, "Even when you miss someone, it's normal for children to laugh and play." (Oh, this is true for grown-ups, too).

Together they decided it would be just fine to talk about their Special Hero whenever they wanted to or needed to. Heartfelt sharing gave a voice to the different thoughts and feelings and helped – a lot.

If one of them felt sad, they could help each other by sharing memories: "outside memories," like favorite songs that he always sang off-key, or "inside memories," like cherishing the ones you love and following your dreams.

When they faced a problem, they could ask themselves or each other, "How would my Special Hero want me to handle this? What kind of advice would he give?"

Now that Greg and Grace had their father's love tucked safely in the pocket of each of their hearts, they still played outdoors, still played games, and still played with their friends.

And still missed their Special Hero.

Lawrence, age 1½

Greg and Grace felt a range of emotions after their Special Hero died. They invite you to use the following HERO PAGE to draw or write about your feelings.

HERO PAGE

Erin, age 8

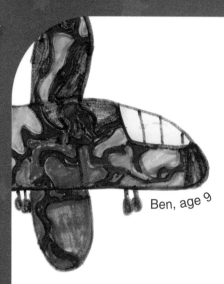
Ben, age 9

Ben, age 9

NAVY.

Chapter 7
Personal Salutes

Using the skills and experience gained as a military family, Greg, Grace, and their mom settled in more and more to their non-military life. In their new bedrooms, Greg and Grace found favorite places to keep their Special Hero camouflage pockets.

They chose the front doorway as the perfect place to display the American flag as a symbol of their patriotic spirit. It wasn't just any American flag, however. It was their father's military funeral flag, which had been folded tightly into a crisp triangle and handed to their mother at the end of the funeral service. Now, everyone who entered their home would know that their dad – their Special Hero – had served our great nation.

Greg hadn't planned on it, but each day as he passed his father's flag he snapped a quick salute. Whenever Grace passed the flag, she reached for her pocket and made a wish.

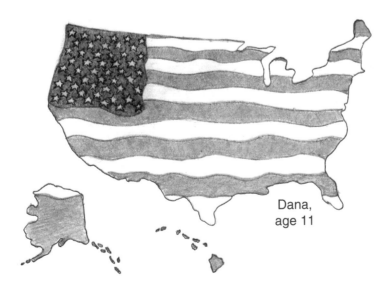

Dana,
age 11

Speaking from the heart, their mom said, "You have memories of your dad now. His life has given you many gifts. As you grow older, you will continue to unwrap the gifts from his life."

With their mother's help, the children wrote letters to different people who knew their father. "We want to know our

Skylar, age 12

dad as you knew him. Please write to us and share a story, and a picture if you have one. We are making a scrapbook to last our whole lives."

Greg and Grace traced the geographical tracks of the letters using their dad's colorful world globe.

One letter was mailed to a family friend who lives on an island near the equator. Another letter was sent to a service member on a submarine somewhere under the sea.

Soon, the postal carrier began delivering what Greg and Grace called the *Remember Letters.* E-mails started arriving, too. Grown-ups wrote they felt better by sharing their memories in a letter, even though they also felt sad about the death.

Skylar, age 12

Each *Remember Letter* presented its own gift. It spoke its own story…in its own voice…in its own unique time, place, and relationship. Greg and Grace learned about their dad, their own Special Hero, for he was also a husband…

A son and a grandson.

> *He was a son-in-law, an uncle, and a brother.*

> *He was a cousin and he was a nephew.*

A student and a teacher.

> *He was a classmate, a teammate, and a roommate.*

> *He was a coach and he was coached.*

A friend and a role model.

> *He was a citizen, a civilian, and a member of the United States Armed Forces.*

> *He was a leader and he was led.*

A battle-buddy…and brave.

Greg and Grace cherished the *Remember Letters* and the pictures, and will for all the years to come. One heartfelt letter became a family favorite.

Dear Greg and Grace,

You must miss your dad an awful lot. If it helps you to know, I do, too. I like your idea of collecting pictures and letters about your dad.

I will always remember serving our country with your father. He was a man of his word. The only thing he loved more than the U.S.A. was his family.

During deployments, a lot of us have personal traditions. Your dad had a curious habit of tapping the pocket of his camouflage jacket. He would tap the pocket lightly but not say anything aloud to anyone.

Tap-tap. Silent Taps.

Well, we never knew what it meant, to whom, or why. I wonder...does it mean something special to you?

Very Respectfully,

J

JLF

P.S. Give my best to your mom.

HERO PAGE

Thara, age 4½

If you could write about or to your Special Hero, what would you like to say?

Photo courtesy of Michael Kitcher

Place a photo here

Photo courtesy of Michael Kircher

Chapter 8
Young Artists

Through their art, these children speak for children everywhere who extend their support to you. Please join me in admiring and appreciating their creativity. Oh, say, can you find all the branches of the U.S. Armed Forces?

Sam, age 8, rides her bike for fun. She misses her dad because of his lengthy recovery at a military hospital far away.

Greg, age 7, always wanted to be a GI Joe. His family's military lineage has been traced back to the Revolutionary War era.

Savannah, age 4½, is the most beautiful princess of playing dress-up. Her grandpa, a retired Army Reserve Command Sergeant Major, agrees.

Skylar, age 12, is an avid reader who also enjoys choreographed gymnastics. Her great-uncles served in WWII.

Lawrence, age 1½, is learning to talk. His cousin is teaching him to say, "Go Army, Beat Navy!"

Ben, age 9, likes playing video games and listening to stories about military life, especially his father's deployment in the Army Reserve.

Emily, age 4, and **Matthew**, age 2, include the troops in their nightly prayers. Their grandfather was in the Marine Corps and also in the Navy.

Carey Rose, age 10, has traveled with her family to Germany, Italy, Switzerland, Austria, Canada, and Ireland. Her dad was stationed in Korea when he was in the Army.

Thara, age 4½, loves arts and crafts. She also enjoys tinkering in the workshop with her grandfather, an inventor.

Erin, age 8, is a budding artist who likes to fly with her dad when he pilots the plane. Her granddaddy was an Air Force pilot.

G. George, age 9, has moved and traveled a lot. His father was stationed in Germany while serving in the military.

Dana, age 11, organized her entire 5th grade class to write letters and send comfort items to U.S. troops. Her grandfather and two great-uncles served for many years in the Merchant Marines.

Sinead, age 10, from an Air Force family, sings in her church choir and likes to visit New York City. Her great-grandmother served in the Merchant Marines.

Alex, age 8, likes to play outdoors with his friends.

Andrew, age 6 ½ plus ¾, is very good at math and loves ice hockey.

Nicole, age 4, likes to play anything that her big brothers are playing!

Alex, Andrew, and Nicole have helped pack care packages for the troops overseas.

Shannon, age 10, is proud of her mom's long career in the Coast Guard. Her father was in the Coast Guard, too. No wonder Shannon's favorite activities are boating and swimming!

Jillian, age 5½, and **Megan**, age 4, are big sisters to baby brother, Jack. They are direct descendants of a Revolutionary War militiaman from the 1st Maryland Regiment. And, their great-great-uncle survived being captured and held as a POW in Germany.

About the Author

The author with the young artist, Savannah

Marlene Lee's volunteer work with injured soldiers and their families inspired her to write *The Hero in My Pocket*. Long dedicated to community service, Marlene was named American Red Cross Volunteer of the Year 2003, Disaster Support Services, National Capital Area (Washington, D.C. metropolitan area). Also in 2003, Marlene developed a community outreach program for injured soldiers and their visiting families; and, in 2004, she was recognized for exceptional volunteer service.

With her son serving as an officer in the U.S. Army and her daughter-in-law holding down the homefront during deployments, Marlene plans to donate a portion of the proceeds from book sales to selected organizations that support military families.

Marlene holds a B.A. in Communications from the University of Maryland and is completing her masters degree in Thanatology at Hood College. During her career at IBM, Marlene received five awards for writing. This is her first children's book.

Megan's portrait of the author